From FEAR *To* LOVE

Your Essential Guide to Parenting Adopted and Foster Children

B. Bryan Post

WORKBOOK

Copyright © Bryan Post 2020

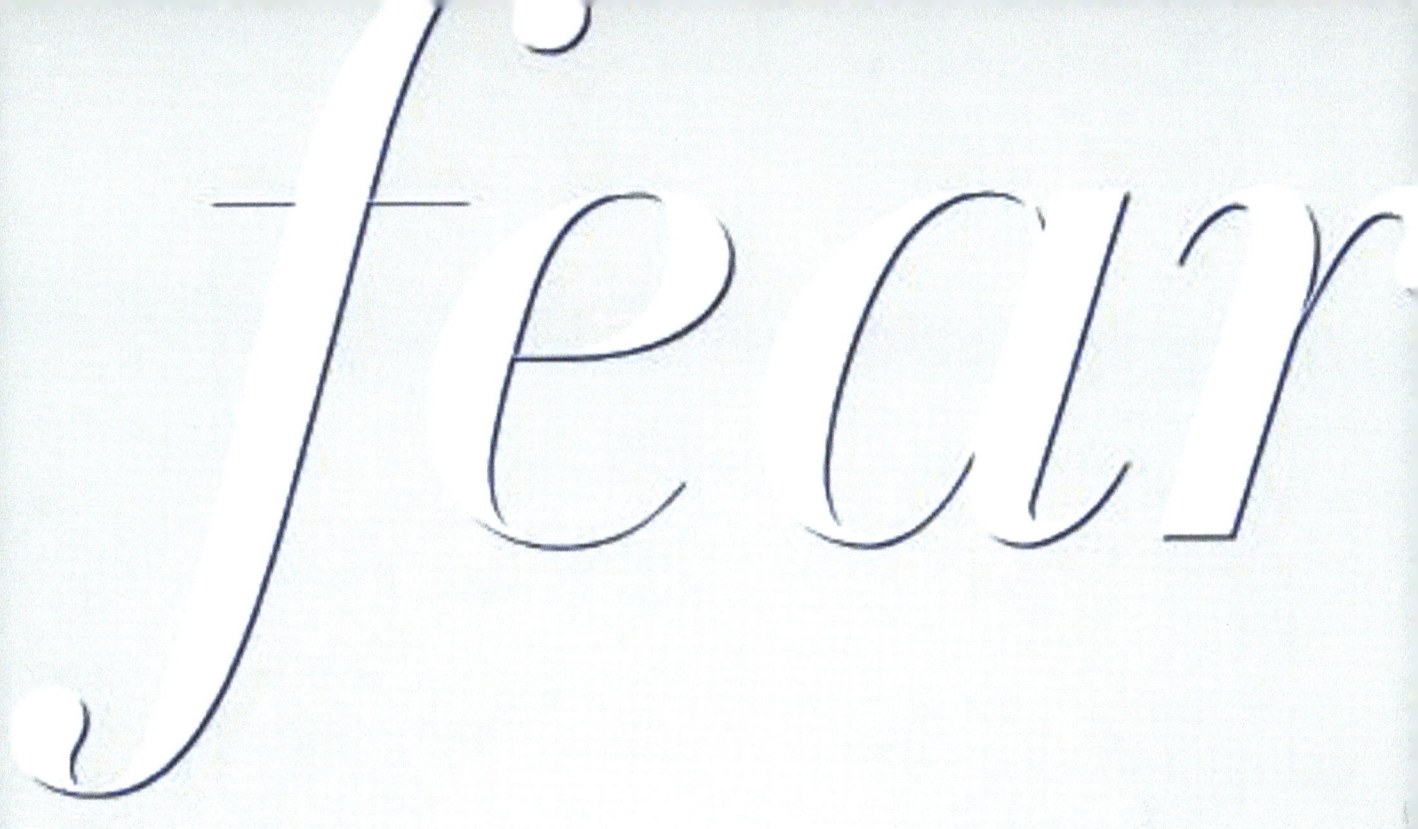

Adoption Clinical Services, LLC
The *FROM FEAR TO LOVE* Training Course

TABLE OF CONTENT

Pre-Test		
Chapter 1	Introduction and Chapter 1	1
Chapter 2:	What Does Stress Have to Do with It	15
Chapter 3:	Don't Underestimate the Role of Trauma	24
Chapter 4:	Regulation and Dysregulation	32
Chapter 5:	The Oxytocin Response	43
Chapter 6:	Ages and Levels of Memory	48
Chapter 7:	Exploring What's Below the Surface	56
Chapter 8:	The Stress Model	59
Chapter 9:	Lying	64
Chapter 10:	Stealing and Self-Mutilation	68
Chapter 11:	Aggressive Behavior	77
Chapter 12:	What do Chronic Lying, Stealing, Fire Setting, Killing Animals, and Hoarding Food Have in Common?	81
Chapter 12:	Feedback Loops	85
Chapter 13:	The 3-Phase Intervention	90
Chapter 14:	Healing Happens at Home	93
	From Fear to Love Conclusion	
Post Test		

GENERAL GUIDELINES

This Training Program is a complement to the book *From Fear to Love*, by Bryan Post. Recommendations for effective learning and utilization of this program involve the following.

- You **MUST** read the book *From Fear to Love*. It will serve as a foundation for growth for you and your family.

- After reading a chapter, review the corresponding section of this Training Program.

- Complete the exercises in each section in their entirety. Be completely honest with yourself. If there is a lack of honesty, you will limit your growth.

- Allow yourself to *feel* through the process. Though it may be difficult, acknowledgment of these feelings will bring you to the positive space necessary to build the relationship between you, your family, and your adopted child.

- Implement the Action Steps and Homework into daily living and track your effectiveness.

- Isolate challenges that occur as you put the systems to use so you can share them with your Parenting Coach. This is a necessary part of the process as it enables you to master those processes and make them a part of your daily routine.

- Above all and with each moment, "Choose Love."

Pre-Test

1. The difference between the Old Paradigm and the New Paradigm is:
a. There is no Old or New Paradigm, there is just parenting, and we all operate differently doing whatever we think is best.
b. The Old Paradigm states that you learned how to parent from your parents and grandparents and the New Paradigm means that you are creating your own new formula for parenting.
c. The Old Paradigm states that you as a parent were in charge and the New Paradigm means that your child is now in charge.
d. The Old Paradigm states that the child is angry and controlling and that as a parent, you are operating from a place of punishment and control; and the New Paradigm means that you, as a parent, are operating from a place of understanding, flexibility, and acceptance.

2. The two primary emotions we feel as human beings are:
a. Love and Anger
b. Love and Hate
c. Love and Fear
d. Love and Jealousy

3. When an adopted child gets stressed:
a. The stress exhausts the child and causes the child to become tired and sleepy.
b. The stress causes confused and distorted thinking and suppresses short-term memory, which then drives negative behavior.
c. The stress causes the child to become clingy.
d. The stress causes the child and parent to immediately come to an understanding, leading to improved behavior.

4. According to the National Institute of Mental Health, stress is:
a. Important to maintain a balanced lifestyle.
b. How the brain and body respond to any demand.
c. A result of our eating habits.
d. Necessary to better manage the behaviors of our children.

5. Stress is _____ and _____ in life.
a. Avoidable and unnecessary
b. Scary and unnecessary
c. A challenge and important
d. Unavoidable and necessary

6. Trauma may occur as early as_____.
a. When a child learns their first words.
b. When a child is first reprimanded.
c. When a child is born.
d. When a child begins to socialize at school.

7. True or False: Trauma is any stressful event that is prolonged, overwhelming, or unpredictable, and when that event continues unexpressed, unprocessed, and misunderstood, it becomes long-term trauma.

8. One step of the healing process is to encourage a conversation with your child. The other two steps are:
a. Listening to your child and then holding them.
b. Explaining to your child the way they should respond and gaining agreement.
c. Explaining to your child why they are reacting badly and brainstorming ideas to improve.
d. Listening to their thoughts and then disciplining through chores.

9. This part of the brain contributes to calming stress and helping a child think more clearly and feel less overwhelmed.
a. Amygdala
b. Hippocampus
c. Orbitofrontal Cortex
d. Sensory Pathway

10. This part of the brain is fully developed at by the time an infant reaches 18 months of age. Therefore, the infant's ability to sense threats, fear, and stress is functioning
a. Amygdala
b. Hippocampus
c. Oxytocin
d. Orbitofrontal Cortex

11. True or False. Oxytocin is called the anti-stress hormone and, sometimes, the bonding hormone because of its power to soothe.

12. Examples of Attuned and Attentive Caregiving, required to initiate the oxytocin response, include all of the following except:

   a. Listening
   b. Hugging
   c. Playing
   d. Ignoring

13. True or False: The oxytocin response is a learned response.

14. True or False: During a time of stress, a child will emotionally revert to an early experience of trauma or the "trauma core."

15. True or False: The State Level is the most difficult level of memory to influence according to traditional perspectives of talk therapy, but when we work from an emotional perspective geared toward the oxytocin response, it isn't true. To influence the State Level, we must create learned responses beyond "talking" that will shift us from a cognitive perspective, to an emotional perspective.

16. The most influential pathways to a child's State Level include all of the following except:

   a. Smiling, seeing a caring face causes the child to experience a sense and feeling of trust.
   b. Addressing an undesirable behavior at the moment a child is triggered
   c. Reflecting back to a child with the same voice and tone intensity of expression or emotion that the child is displaying.
   d. Voice tone, which can help to calm a child's state level of memory depending on the level of the child's triggered state.

17. True or False. Regulation helps you to stay calm and focused. It enables you to manage your emotions, minimizing your fears and creating understanding with your child.

18. True or False. Dysregulation is the body's state of stress outside the window of tolerance. Dysregulation is a place where you see things clearly and translate thoughts in a lucid, practical manner.

19. True or False. The Stress Model™ purports that all behavior arises from a state of stress. It is through the expression, the processing, and the understanding of the fear that we can calm the stress and diminish the behavior.

20. The 3-Step Formula to Respond Vs React includes all of the following except:

   a. Stop and think. Do you know why your child is behaving the way they are?
   b. Assume the reason for the negative behavior based on previous experience.
   c. Take 3 to 10 deep breaths.
   d. Respond either with a question or statement

21. True or False. The formula for helping a child overcome lying is to ignore the lie but don't ignore the child because when you ignore the lie, you're ignoring the child's fear and stress state.

22. True or False. Learning occurs when the child moves out of the stress state, their thinking is clearer, and their short-term memory becomes available.

23. True or False. Stealing and self-mutilation are not addictive behaviors

24. A primary step in managing self-mutilation behavior is to reinforce your support by doing all of the following except:
a. Saying, "Cut yourself if you need to, but I would really like for you to come and tell me when you feel like you need to cut yourself so I can be there for you."
b. Being physically and mentally present when it happens to reduce the child's stress.
c. Coming from a place of understanding and listening.
d. Asking the child, "What's the matter with you?" This will force the child to stop.

25. Aggressive behaviors include all of the following except:
a. Sharing your feelings.
b. Cursing.
c. Punching and kicking walls.
d. Attacking a person or animal.

26. True or False. As long as a child is in a state of stress and fear, he cannot develop secure attachment. As long as the parents are in states of fear and stress, they can't bond with the child. Attachment and bonding is a two-way street.

27. True or False. According to the Stress Model™, parental regulation is ultimately the single most important factor in the development of successful independent regulatory functioning in children to bring the child from dysregulation to regulation.

28. All of the following are examples of Cognitive Behavior Parenting Tools, except:
a. Excessive
b. Chores
c. Isolation
d. Listening

29. Which of the following is NOT an example of a Negative Feedback Loop?
a. "You're going to do it because I said so!"
b. "Don't you talk to me like that!"
c. "Wow, what's going on here?"
d. "You just wait until your dad gets home, and we'll see what happens!"

30. Which is not an example of a parenting response from a Positive Feedback Loop:
a. "Wow, what's going on?"
b. "Misbehaving isn't going to solve this."
c. "Something must really be bothering you."
d. "Can we talk about what just happened here

31. One way to create a Positive Feedback Loop is:
a. Reflect, Relate Regulate
b. Reflect, Remember, Relate
c. Peace, Love, and Harmony
d. Research, Remember, Recover

32. The steps of the Positive Feedback Loop include all of the following except:
a. Reflect: Take 3-10 deep breaths
b. Remember your objective.
c. Relate to your child.
d. Regulate yourself, your child, and the environment.

33. True or False. Mindfulness is one of the most important tools a parent can use to maintain their own state of calm and regulation to better influence and parent a child. It is the ability to slow down enough to watch your own thoughts, sensations, perceptions, and behaviors.

34. In-home healing opportunities include all of the following except:
a. Time In Versus Time Out
b. Containment
c. Affection Prescription
d. Regulate

Chapter 1

Introduction and Chapter 1

In this section, you will learn:

- The difference between the Old Paradigm and the New Paradigm and how it will help you view your child authentically

- The two primary emotions we feel as human beings

- What happens to the thinking of an adopted child when stressed?

- The greatest struggle in your relationship with your adopted child and how to manage it

- The difference between perceived "love" with the Old Paradigm and "love" with the New Paradigm

What is a paradigm? It's a pattern from which you shape and live your life. Dictionary.com defines it as "A set of assumptions, concepts, values, and practices that constitutes a way of viewing reality for the community that shares them…"

Examples of paradigms may be:

- What are breakfast foods?

- What time do you have breakfast?

- What clothes are appropriate to wear for work?

- What side of the road do you drive on?

With the above responses, your answers may be direct, and in your mind, a fact. However, in other parts of the world, where people may operate by a different paradigm, it's not that way. This same theory applies to parenting. We learned a set way to parent - to use discipline and to punish, and we believe it is the right and only way to parent. In fact, it's not.

EMOTION, LOVE, AND FEAR

Let's examine emotion. Emotion is energy in motion. Though we've grown up to believe we have a ton of emotions, in fact, we have only two. The two *primary* emotions are love and fear.

Let's review. A "feeling" is the cognitive perception of an emotional state. This means that your brain translates its perception of the energy shift into a feeling. So, your brain takes your emotion of love or fear and interprets it as "I feel happy," "I feel angry," "I feel jealous," and so forth. Many people find this difficult to grasp because our tendency is to believe that anger is a primary emotion. Anger, however, stems from fear. Hate stems from fear. Jealousy stems from fear. On the other hand, when it comes to love, caring stems from love, understanding stems from love, acceptance comes from love. To summarize, we have only two states: thriving (love) and surviving (fear).

OLD PARENTING PARADIGM:

The old paradigm says that the difficult child is angry and controlling and that as parents, we must respond with discipline to teach the child a lesson. We say things like, "I'm giving you this whipping because I love you and want you to learn." Or, "I'm sending you to your room without dinner because you have to learn about manners and respect. If I didn't love you, I wouldn't care." We learned that love was spanking, yelling, control, force, power, and punishment. This is the Old Paradigm of parenting and is really our own *fear* in disguise.

BELOW THE SURFACE OF THE OLD PARENTING PARADIGM:

The reality of the old parenting paradigm is that this child is caught in a stress-and-fear state, which causes the body's natural fear reaction to go awry. This resembles bad behavior with your adopted child. Truthfully, the fetus, infant, or child is the product of an overly stressful environment or traumatic event, causing fearfulness and stress sensitivity. Bottom line, the adopted child acts out.

Neurobiologist Bruce Lipton says, "During times of stress, the cellular system constricts into survival, and then every cell in the body is in a state of fear." Stress can occur through any sensory pathway. There are actually nine sensory pathways.

Can you guess all nine?

1. Sight
2. Sound
3. Smell
4. Touch
5. Taste

These are the most common ones and most oft cited.

Yet there are four more that impact us to the same and varying degrees:
6. Movement
7. Digestion
8. Temperature
9. Intuition

The significance of your sensory pathways is that they are unconscious. They cause your body to react to sensory input below consciousness; therefore, you can become stressed and never even know why.

Your child, just like you, can become stressed without even knowing why.

Take a minute and write beside each sensory pathway an example of it becoming activated without "consciously" being aware of it.

1. Sight:
2. **Sound**:
3. Smell:
4. Touch:
5. Taste:
6. Movement:
7. Digestion:
8. Temperature:
9. Intuition:

Joseph LeDoux, author of *The Emotional Brain*, states that "stress causes confused and distorted thinking and suppresses short-term memory." The most common example of this is when you are talking to a friend, and you try to remember the name of someone. At that moment, you cannot do it. For the life of you, you cannot remember that name. But an hour later, it pops into your head. That's because at the moment, you become stressed and your immediate short-term recall is suppressed.

For adopted children with trauma histories, this experience can often be much more intense.

A mother can say to an adopted child, "Sorry, honey, Mama is busy right now and cannot play." A simple enough statement. Unless you are a child with a history of abandonment. This simple statement has the potential to be perceived as a threat. The brain then escalates into stress making the child feel as though the mother must no longer love them since she is unwilling to play. This shuts down the short-term memory the child has of the mother's endearing love and how they normally play every day. Because the child is stressed and the short-term memory is suppressed, she can feel overtaken with fear, which then drives negative behavior.

Give an example of when this happened to you as a child.

Describe a situation when this happened with your child.

This affects our response as a parent. If you are caught in the Old Paradigm, you too are living in fear — fear of not gaining control of your child, fear of what your child may become, fear that your child will not live a full, happy life. This fear causes the greatest struggle in your relationship with your child.

Harold and Edna Crawford were the first Healing Home parents assigned at Adoption Clinical Services, Inc. approximately 15 years ago. Their first assignment was a 17-year-old girl. She had a highly explosive personality. Her first words to Harold and Edna were "I'm not staying here with these m———- f———s." And she continued with expletives. It shocked both Harold and Edna. Harold immediately fell back to the old parenting paradigm. Words like "Don't you roll your eyes at me.

I will knock you into next week. Shake your head one more time and I'll knock it off." Sound familiar? Harold knew, though, that would accomplish nothing. After regulating himself, he used phrases like, "You seem really angry. Why are you so angry? I'd be angry too. I'm angry for you." He heard her. He listened. He participated in her stress, and she calmed down. He knew she liked basketball and asked if she wanted to go out to play basketball. They did. That explosive incident never happened again.
Over 15 years later, that girl is their forever daughter.

EXERCISES

What are five core values and beliefs your parents instilled upon you? (Consider inner values like honesty, loyalty, hard work, faithfulness, persistence, care for others, integrity, etc.)

1.

2.

3.

4.

5.

What is your most positive memorable event as a child? How has that affected you today?

What is your most negative memorable event as a child? How has that affected you today?

List three situations where you were disciplined as a child? How were you disciplined? In what ways has that affected you today?

Describe the last situation where you disciplined your child? (If it was not the first occurrence, share the various ways you disciplined your child.)

THE NEW PARENTING PARADIGM

Let's look at the New Paradigm for parenting. If you are now aware that a difficult adopted child is caught in a stress-and-fear state, which means they are acting out in "fear," and if you are now increasingly more aware and conscious of your own fear, you now can move into love—*and react in love*. This is easier said than done.

Love is the most powerful parenting space in which to live. In this space, you
can more readily see the fear of your child rather than a perception of willful disobedience, and you will address situations in accordance. Instead of saying, "Stop that or you're on a time out," you'll be more likely to say, "You're really mad. What got you so mad? I would be mad too. I would be angry too. It's okay that you're angry."

This means you are more steadily operating from love in the relationship. You are operating from a place of understanding, flexibility, acceptance, tolerance, patience, and faithfulness. Now you are shifting from the Old Paradigm to the
New Paradigm. The below *Word Identifying Markers* are your cues for progress. As you interact with your adopted child, track each time you find yourself in the New Paradigm vs. the Old Paradigm.

Please remember, this is a process of moving from the Old Paradigm to the New Paradigm. It doesn't happen overnight. It is something learned, practiced, refined, practiced, refined, practiced, and so on. There will be mistakes. Mistakes are apart of life and that's okay. And remember, this is why we have the words, "I'm sorry." They are a wonderful addition and symbol o our growth, not failure.

Old and New Paradigm "Word Identifying Markers"

Old Paradigm	New Paradigm
Fear Disguised as Love	**Love**
Spanking	Understanding
Yelling	Flexibility
Control	Acceptance
Force	Tolerance
Punishment	Patience
Faithfulness	

Are there other words you might add to these lists?

Below are examples of phrases not to use, the Old Parenting Paradigm, and phrases to use, the New Parenting Paradigm. As a parent learns more about this love-based approach to therapy, you will become creative in coming up with your own language of regulation.

Phrases Not to Use (Old Paradigm):
- I told you a thousand times not to do that.
- You are hard-headed.
- You will be just like your daddy.
- You're bad.
- Don't lie to me.
- Tell the truth.

Phrases to Use (New Paradigm):
- It's okay, honey, people make mistakes.
- I know sometimes I don't explain myself clearly.
- I'm sorry your parents are not here, but I'm your parent now and I love you.
- Honey, it's okay, some bad things happened to you, that's why you do the things you do.
- Son, it really disappoints me when you lie to me, then walk away.

EXERCISES:

Consider three times when a parent or adult understood you. Perhaps it was even a teacher or a grandparent. Tell the story below. How did it make you feel? How did it impact you as you grew up?

Describe the last time you operated from a place of love with your adopted child. A time when you acted in understanding, flexibility, acceptance, tolerance, patience, and faithfulness. What resulted from that interaction?

What 3 things will you do differently moving forward in the New Paradigm? What phrases will you incorporate into your daily living?

Chapter 2

What Does Stress Have to Do with It

In this section, you will learn:

- What is stress?

- Stress is an unavoidable and necessary part of life.

- How stress impacts us and our adopted children.

- Stress will cause a hypo- or hyper-aroused state in your child.
- Children who have experienced trauma will have a significantly different reaction to stress than children who have not.

WHAT IS STRESS?

According to the National Institute of Mental Health, "Stress is how the brain and body respond to any demand."

There are two things to consider regarding stress. Stress is unavoidable and stress is necessary in our lives. That's right! We cannot avoid stress because it keeps us healthy. Imagine a security alarm system. It exists to alert the homeowner of a break-in. Stress works in a similar fashion. It lets us know that something is going on with our bio-electrochemical system, our body. The same as if we ingested food that was spoiled. Our body goes into a stress state, which manifests itself as a stomachache and we do something to calm the condition. Likewise, trauma causes the body to go into a stress state, which causes the person to act (consciously or unconsciously) in ways to calm the stress.

POSITIVE STRESS AND NEGATIVE STRESS

Let's explore the two types of stress: Positive Stress and Negative Stress.

Positive Stressors can motivate and excite us and even improve our performance. Positive Stressors are within our ability to cope. Negative Stressors can cause anxiety, mental and physical problems, and can demotivate us. Negative Stressors can be outside of our ability to cope.

Examples of Positive Stressors

- Promotion
- New Job
- Divorce
- Vacation
- Holidays

Examples of Negative Stressors

- Loss of a loved one
- Abuse
- Divorce
- Injury
- Job Loss
- Relationship problems

Positive stressors such as public speaking, one of America's greatest fears, even as an adult, may cause you to act out. Sales Representatives were tested in this manner.

Prior to performing their sales presentation in front of their peers, they became agitated, aggressive, sarcastic, and even passive-aggressive. Stress, good or bad, may bring out the worst in anyone.

Now, let's look at an adopted child who has experienced trauma. Trauma heightens the child's responses and reactions to stress, making these children fearful and stress-sensitive, which may cause difficult behavior problems. Trauma could express itself as a number of behaviors that might include anti-social behavior, the inability to form healthy attachments, acting out sexually to calm the stress, bullying, lying, stealing, and apathy, to name a few. Adoptive children experience a lot of stress because of the internalized dynamics of rejection and abandonment stimulated in utero, plus the array of other negative events that might occur after birth.

Bruce Perry, a preeminent neuroscientist, who has conducted some of the most important work regarding children and trauma, says that we all respond to stress in one of two ways: by becoming hypo-aroused or hyper-aroused. Hyper-arousal leads to hyperactivity, agitation, and/or aggression. For example, "Child A" has a chronic trauma history. Child A is also homeschooled. One morning, she realized the other two youth living in the home were not going to school. Child A became immediately angry. She cursed and threatened the other youth. The stressor for Child A was that she would not be home alone, as she thought she would. The trauma was triggered by the other youth being in the home.

Seventy percent of children will respond to most parenting styles, but the other 30% don't respond well to the Old Paradigm of parenting. Adopted and traumatized children fall within the 30%. Bio-children typically have brains that are better equipped to handle stress than adopted children.

Now let's look at hypo-arousal. Hypo-arousal leads to withdrawal, depression, and perhaps resistance. "Child B" has a good-natured, happy, loving personality. However, another child in the home was angry and threatened Child B. Child B became quiet and non-responsive. After the incident, a parent asked Child B if she was okay. Child B responded, "Yes," and went to her room. The parent thought everything was okay until the parent heard a loud crash and glass breaking. The parent went into Child B's room, and they found that Child B had thrown her radio through a window. Child B in a hypo-aroused state.

The behaviors of hypo- and hyper-arousal in adopted children are greatly heightened as compared to other children. However, there are a few key phrases you may find helpful. A parent will not know if a child goes into a hypo-aroused state unless the parent understands the state. A child with hypo-arousal tendencies should not be left alone after a triggering event.

Possible Responses for Children/Hypo-Aroused State
I'm sorry that happens to you. I'm glad you're safe.
Wow, that was scary.
I will sit with you for a while to make sure you stay safe.

Possible Responses for Children/Hyper-Aroused State
I know you are angry, it's okay.
I would be angry too if (DESCRIBE SITUATION)
Tell me how angry you are.
I got a little scared and want to be sure you're safe.

EXERCISES

Based on the positive stressors listed above, what was the last positive stressful situation you experienced in your life? What behaviors, persons, and words helped you manage the stress effectively?

How would you have responded to the situation if you were criticized or punished for your stress-based reactions?

Based on the negative stressors listed above, what was the last negative stress you experienced in your life? What behaviors, persons, and words helped you manage the stress effectively?

How would you have responded to the situation if you were criticized or punished for your stress-based reactions?

What negative stressors has your child been through that you are aware of? Abuse, neglect, continuous moving in and out of homes, sexual abuse?

What behaviors is your child exhibiting now that cause you to punish him/her?

Knowing that trauma in adopted children causes defiance, list your child's challenging behavior and rate on a scale of 1-5 what you would perceive as your child's level of stress?

Behaviors	Rate Their Level of Stress (Scale 1-5, with 5 being the highest)

Knowing that your child is stress-sensitive, what might be something you can you say or do to help alleviate their stress?

When your child becomes hypo-aroused, what will you do differently?

When your child becomes hyper-aroused, what will you do differently?

Chapter 3:

Don't Underestimate the Role of Trauma

In this section you will learn:

- What is trauma?

- Learn how to honor your child's feelings without allowing your own fears to impede the healing process.

- Three things you can do as your child works through the healing process.

- The three types of trauma: traumatic stress, shock trauma, and developmental trauma.

- The two types of trauma that are most widely associated with adoptive children.

- The part of our brain responsible for our physiological reaction to fear and that "gut feeling" you get.

- What control really means and why it's so important to recognize it.

WHAT IS TRAUMA

What is trauma? Trauma is any stressful event that is prolonged, overwhelming, or unpredictable, and when that event continues unexpressed, unprocessed, and misunderstood, it becomes long-term trauma.

WHEN TRAUMA BEGIN

So, what is the source of trauma? Trauma may occur as early as birth. The birth process is traumatic for a child simply because the child is separated from his or her biological mother. This baby has heard its mother's heartbeat, voice, and even smelled her scent for nine consecutive months. Suddenly, outside of the womb and with its adoptive mother, everything familiar is gone. And sadly, it will never be there again. When an adopted child is taken away from his or her biological mother, a grief reaction is created within the baby's body-mind system, and the physiology is disrupted.

Considering the Old Parenting Paradigm, as the child grows, often adoptive parents will view their adopted child's grief or longing for their biological parent as some parental shortcoming on their part. This is yet another error in judgment and more so reflects the adoptive parents' own insecurities and fear than anything else. Typically, there is an abundance of mixed feelings, but they all arise from your own fear.

EXERCISE

What are you feeling regarding your child's grief and loss of their biological parent? Does it make you feel guilty, sad, or angry?

HEALING FOR YOUR ADOPTIVE CHILD

As you accept your own feelings, give your child permission to accept their feelings. One way to do this is through talking. Talking gives your child permission to grieve. Grief is a natural and necessary element in your adopted child's growth process.

Too often, we simply don't permit it to happen because we make well-intentioned but invalidating statements such as, "Well, Honey, I love you, and if your mother hadn't allowed you to be adopted, I would never have met you," or "But you're my child now; aren't I enough for you?" Worse yet are statements such as, "Why would you want your mother back or cry for her? She gave you away!" Such statements do nothing to help your child heal. They reflect your own insecurities. Honor those feelings for yourself, but don't let your fear impede your child's own healing process. It's the only way to help your child get past the trauma of losing his or her biological parents.

THE 3 STEPS OF THE HEALING PROCESS

Encourage + Listen + Support

ENCOURAGE the conversation. The below statements can encourage a conversation between you and your adopted child.

"Honey, I can understand why you would feel that way." "It's very natural to have those feelings; I'll bet they are very sad ones." "I'm listening. It's okay."

LISTEN: Effective listening is key.

- Be attentive.
- Don't interrupt.
- Don't finish your child's sentences.
- Clarify your child's responses for understanding.
- Ask questions.

SUPPORT.

- Hold your child tightly.
- Rock your child.
- Rub your child's back.
- Thank your child for sharing their thoughts and feelings.

No matter what your child asks or says, remember, you don't need to have all the answers. When the grieving process can finally begin, it will work itself through in time, and your adopted child can heal and fully allow you to love him or her without resistance.

EXERCISE

What can you do to improve in each of these areas?
ENCOURAGE:

LISTEN:

SUPPORT:

TRAUMA: HOW DEEP DOES IT GO?

Adoption—both pre-adoption and post-adoption—is a traumatic experience.

Pre-adoption trauma triggers would include birth trauma, drug abuse, rejection, violence, and malnutrition. Post-adoption trauma triggers often include situations such as abuse, neglect, and frequent moves. Adoptive children have usually experienced two of the three traumas described below.

THE THREE KINDS OF TRAUMA

1. Traumatic Stress, which includes neglect or physical, sexual, or emotional abuse (Would birth trauma and drug abuse and malnutrition be in here?

2. Shock Trauma, which includes bombs, car accidents, earthquakes, and any other immediate, unavoidable events

3. Developmental Trauma is any trauma that occurs during the childhood stages.

Traumatic Stress and Developmental Trauma are the two traumas most often experienced in children pre-adoption and post-adoption.

EXERCISE

Please refer to Page 12 in the book *From Fear to Love*. Here Bryan Post shares a story of a boy who is encopretic. Please review the story and answer these questions:

What about that story did you relate to regarding your adopted child?

What does this story teach you about the depth trauma can affect a life?

What was the boy's trauma based upon?

What three things does Bryan suggest doing?

The Old Paradigm is that her son's behavior was angry, controlling, and manipulative. What we fail to understand is that we're all controlling and manipulative when we're scared. When we try to exert control, it's a survival mechanism. *If I'm stressed out and scared, I feel desperate to get some control.*

EXERCISES

Think of a recent time in your life when life seemed out of control. In what ways did you try to gain control? (Consider stressful situations like job loss, financial issues, or weight loss.)

When life settled, how did your need to control change? How were you different?

What behavior does your child demonstrate when scared and life seems out of control?

What will you do to help them feel safe?

Chapter 4:

REGULATION AND DYSREGULATION

In this section, you will learn:

- What is Regulation and why it serves as a defining moment in an adopted child's life.

- What is Dysregulation and how it relates to difficult, challenging adopted children.

- How we limit our child's growth if we, as parents, are not regulated.

- What is Amygdala Hijacking and how it relates to Dysregulation?

- How the hippocampus impacts our behaviors and why it needs to be functioning effectively.

- What you can do as an adoptive parent to regenerate the hippocampus so the child's response to stress will moderate.

IMPORTANT DEVELOPMENTAL TERMS

AMYGDALA. The Amygdala plays a key role in the processing of emotions. It is part of your emotional brain and "online" at birth. Its growth rate is equal to the brain stem. By the time an infant reaches 18 months of age, the amygdala is fully developed. Therefore, the infant's ability to sense threats, fear, and stress is functioning.

HIPPOCAMPUS. The hippocampus is the part of the brain that contributes to calming stress and helping a child think more clearly and feel less overwhelmed. It doesn't complete its development until the 36th month of life. This is important because it establishes a neurologic basis for why we shouldn't allow babies to cry themselves to sleep. It's too stressful for their developing brain structure. It leads to stressed and overly sensitive babies. So, if possible, when helping your child settle in for naps and at night, lie down with him or her until they fall asleep. This will help them to learn to regulate their internal state for sleep through your influence. It's important to understand that a baby can't soothe itself. There is a bio-energetic natural rhythm between mother and baby that begins at fertilization of the female egg. Through this natural bio-energetic rhythm, the baby learns how to soothe him/herself learned through the interaction between mother and baby, through the release of oxytocin (The Relationship Hormone). Trauma interrupts this natural occurrence, which causes a disruption in the baby's ability to self soothe him/herself. When a parent or caregiver is in a place of regulation, lying down with a child will help them to regulate and fall asleep. Remember that a baby is coming from a place of stress. As parents, we calm the stress. We nurture the baby and by doing so, teach the baby to soothe itself.

We've mentioned that allowing a baby to cry is not ideal because the baby encounters far too much stress, to begin with. What other stresses does a baby encounter?
Please review Chapter 4 for suggestions and ideas.

What can you do to best support your adopted child, considering each issue listed above?

ORBITOFRONTAL CORTEX. The orbitofrontal cortex is the social and emotional control center of the brain, the part of our brain that is most readily responsible for how we get along in society. This part of our brain does not completely develop until we are 25 years old! Considering we call 18-year-olds adults, this is seven years before a brain is neurologically equipped to function as an adult. The orbitofrontal cortex is one of the only areas of the brain open to change throughout our lifespan. So, if we are breathing, there is hope for change.

In summary, never give up on your children because you never know when some developmental milestone will be met that will help them better learn the most appropriate dynamics for social and emotional living.

REGULATION, DYSREGULATION, THE AMYGDALA, THE HIPPOCAMPUS, AND THE ORBITOFRONTAL CORTEX

Imagine a fight with your significant other where you both fly off the handle. You're tired of them being late and they're tired of you not understanding their schedule. What does this behavior accomplish? Probably nothing if everyone is in a state of Dysregulation. Even if one of you were in a state of Regulation, something could be accomplished. It's the same with your adopted child. When your adopted child is difficult or demanding, this drives your own fears, which may cause anger toward the child to stop what they are doing. You are BOTH in a state of Dysregulation.

The child is acting out and we snap to a punishment. However, when we are calm and in control of our feelings, we can see things more clearly and ultimately come from a place of love and understanding. In doing this, we are now living the new Parenting Paradigm. Let's look closely at Regulation and Dysregulation.

WHAT IS REGULATION?

Regulation deals with "affect regulation," the regulation of the emotional state and behavior. It is like balancing on a seesaw. You might get stressed out, but if you can stay in balance, you don't become too angry or too sad. That's regulation within your window of tolerance—the degree of stress that you can tolerate without getting out of balance. Regulation helps you to stay calm and focused. In essence, Regulation enables you to manage your emotions, so it minimizes your fears and creates understanding of the opposition. Here, the opposition is your child. When you manage or regulate your own fears so you can be a source of support to your adopted child, you diminish their stress, which opens their mind to growth and development. If a child is in dysregulation, they may act out, hurt another child during play and misbehave. When instances like this occur, you may see a teacher or parent pull the child aside and sit with them, thereby minimizing or eliminating the stress. The goal is to get the child to a play of regulation. Once a child is regulated, the child can be involved in regular age-appropriate activities. Without these regulatory abilities, a child will suffer throughout every day.

WHAT IS DYSREGULATION

Dysregulation is the body's state of stress outside the window of tolerance; you move outside your body-mind's ability to tolerate the stress. The story about the fight with your significant other exemplifies two people in a state of dysregulation. It's a place where you cannot see things clearly and are unable to translate thoughts in a lucid, practical manner.

Difficult and challenging adopted children are chronically dysregulated and struggling with their ability to self-regulate. Earlier, we learned of a 17-year old with an explosive personality. As a baby, she was found in an abandoned building almost starved to death. After being rescued, she was in numerous foster homes and a failed adoptive home, where she was abused. This child did not receive the nurturing that a baby needs to learn self-regulation. Therefore, she could not regulate herself. With this, she had not learned a healthy oxytocin release, so high levels of cortisol were released when stress was triggered.

Dr. Perry refers to this state in children as an "amygdala hijacking." As soon as the amygdala senses a threat through a sensory pathway, it has a reaction. Sensory pathways are defined as what we see, smell, hear, touch, taste, or feel— or even body temperature.

SENSORY PATHWAY/TRIGGER

For example, "seeing." A child may be used to seeing a parent's stoic flat face that resulted in trouble for the child. Should the child come into contact with someone else who demonstrates that same facial expression, the child may end up in the same state of dysregulation. The child's eyes are conditioned to react to that same facial expression. "Smell" can produce the same state of dysregulation. If a child smelled a cigar while being molested, they can associate a cigar smell with the experience and find themselves in a state of dysregulation. If "hearing" a strong tone of voice has led to physical abuse in the past, the child may associate that tone in another situation even though a person poses no threat.

With amygdala hijacking, the amygdala senses a threat in the environment, like the story about the boy who pooped in his pants every time he had to deal with a transition and pumps out these important stress hormones, which go to the pituitary gland and make their way to the hippocampus. The hippocampus is the amygdala's modulator because the hippocampus helps us to think clearly in stressful situations. In stress, however, the hippocampus has a hard time doing its job properly, so our short-term memory is affected in times of overwhelming stress and our thinking processes become confused and distorted. So, children in a chronic state of dysregulation are confused. In a previous example, we discussed a child who asked his mother to play, but she had something important to do. The child cannot understand this situation is isolated, that his mother plays with him all the time. He just feels abandoned. If his mother is aware of the situation, she can reassure the child that they are safe and will have playtime tomorrow. This constant reassurance will help the child regulate situations like this.

When this state of stress is prolonged and overwhelming, stress research shows that neuronal damage can occur in the hippocampus. The hippocampus can even develop new neuronal connections that make a child more sensitive. An example of this is a child who experiences the suicide of his mother, but never processes his feelings and thoughts with anyone about it and is plagued with what the psychological community describes as abnormal behaviors. This child may develop a hypersensitivity to sound, sensation, or urges. It's a survival mechanism, but it builds in an ultimately destructive way.

If the amygdala is being triggered, it is learning that it must stay on alert all the time. In this heightened state of alert, the amygdala is exercised more, and the hippocampus breaks down. The child's ability to focus suffers; the child's ability to regulate suffers, and the child's ability to relate to others in a positive way suffers. Ultimately, adopted children exhibiting difficult behaviors often struggle in relationships.

EXERCISE

Describe a time where you flew off the handle? Who were you talking to? What resulted from that situation?

Describe a time where cool heads prevailed? What specifically happened? What made this situation different?

When was the last time you reacted in anger toward your adopted child due to their behavior? How did your child respond? What did you accomplish?

HEALING THE HIPPOCAMPUS

There are two ways to change the brain: positive environment and positive relationships, plus the positive repetition of both. When stress is interrupted for prolonged periods, the hippocampus can regenerate. The orbitofrontal cortex—the social and emotional control center—is one of the few brain areas open for change and development throughout our life spans.

Let's discuss the 17-year old girl with an explosive personality. Whenever she became triggered, she'd walk around threatening to beat up the other kids in the house. Because of her intensity, we took the other children out of the house. However, she continued to curse and threaten the parent. The parent incorporated the same behavior into the girl's therapy—yelling back at the girl. The parent's yelling, though, was a support to the girl. When the girl expressed why she was angry, the parent would yell back, "Somebody f———d you up, but it wasn't me." "I'd be angry too." "You should be angry." "Tell me more." "I'm here because I care about you. I want you to be safe." "I'm sorry somebody treated you like that, but I'm here to care about you." Gradually, the girl calmed down. The parent started this process regulated and matched the girl's anger in a supportive way. As the girl calmed down, the parent continued to mirror the girl and calmed down as well. Later, the girl went to the bedroom for a short period. When she came out, she asked to play basketball as if nothing ever happened. Together, the parent and the girl played basketball.

For parents to know what to do in a relationship with their child, the parent must first understand themselves and the parenting paradigm they parent from. The parent must first work on themselves, get to a place of regulation, and then they are in the best place to help their child.

What does a Positive Environment and a Positive Relationship Look Like?

If we looked closely at being in a state of regulation, you are in a place where your own issues do not interfere with the reactions you are getting from your child. You are not living in fear of how your child is behaving or the potential outcome of their behavior. You are merely listening to your child, allowing their feelings to count, asking questions to them about why they may be behaving the way they are. You are being mindful of yourself and being in tune with what they are feeling.

Remember, it doesn't mean you feel nothing, you do. But you can put your issues in a place so you can be there for your child. You are in an untainted space with your child that allows them to grow and take steps toward regulation.

EXERCISES

Based on the above paragraph and the Positive Environment and Relationship elements, what are you doing well? Where can you improve?

What can you do for your child now? Where can you improve?

Chapter 5:
THE OXYTOCIN RESPONSE

In this section, you will learn:

- What is Oxytocin and how does it help our body's stress response system?
- How a lack of attentive care giving prevents the Oxytocin response from managing chronic stress, abuse, or neglect.
- The positive effects of attuned and attentive care on the Oxytocin response.
- The importance of apologizing.
- That pressure for accomplishment, consequences, behavior modification, and traditional punishment practices creates minimal opportunities for the Oxytocin response to kick in.

What is Oxytocin?

Oxytocin is called the anti-stress hormone and, sometimes, the bonding hormone because of its power to soothe. When the stress hormones pass through the hypothalamus, it's supposed to turn on the oxytocin response, flooding the body simultaneously with oxytocin. *Research has discovered that the oxytocin response is a learned response. It doesn't just occur naturally.*

Attuned and attentive caregiving is required to initiate the oxytocin response. Without attuned and attentive caregiving, the response doesn't become adequately conditioned in the face of chronic stress, abuse, or emotional absence. So, an adopted child might grow up with a poorly developed oxytocin response system, making the child prone to prolonged states of stress, high anxiety, aggression, depression, and an abundance of other emotional triggers.

With attuned and attentive caregiving, however, your adopted child will have a healthy oxytocin response and can better engage in healthy social and emotional relationships. IT IS A MUST and the biggest breakthrough in parenting history in creating healthy attachment. This means you are helping your child become more regulated, develop secure relationships, and feel happier. The bottom line is that oxytocin is critical.

Every action toward a child must be geared toward turning on that child's oxytocin response. Below, please find a list of a few simple things you can do to provide attuned and attentive are giving and turn on your child's oxytocin response.

When was the last time you did the following? What was the situation? How did your child respond?

Smiling:

Being present:

Listening:

Hugging:

Holding:

Rocking:

Playing:

Sharing meals:

Laughing:

Massaging:

Patience:

Making eye contact:

Encouraging:

How will you incorporate the above more readily into your day? Define specific situations?

When was the last time you did any of the below? What was the situation? What resulted from your actions?

ACTIONS TO AVOID

Shaming:

Blaming:

Threatening:

Yelling:

Making Demands:

What will you do to avoid these actions in the future and instead activate your child's oxytocin response?

BEST PRACTICE WHEN YOU MESS UP?

Go to the child and sincerely apologize.

When was the last time you apologized to someone? Who was it and what was the situation? Was it sincere? How did they respond?

When was the last time you sincerely apologized to your child? What was the situation?

Chapter 6:
AGES AND LEVELS OF MEMORY

In this section you will learn:

- What is a Trauma Barrier and how does it affect us when dealing with stress?
- What are the four levels of memory that impact how we react to the world.

During a time of stress, a child will emotionally revert to an early experience of trauma or the "trauma barrier." Research says that adults can revert to infancy when under high levels of stress. Recently a young lady called for counseling relating to a situation with her fiancé. She said that she cooked corn tortillas for him. His response was that he doesn't eat corn tortillas. She got so angry that she left the house and sat at the bottom of the steps of their apartment building, in the cold. As we talked, she said that when she had to care for her sisters, they ate whatever she gave them. She became triggered because of a childhood experience. The result was that she got angry and pouted like a little kid, which resulted in her storming out of the house and sitting in the cold.

Likewise, let's look at a 13-year-old who acts like a 3-year-old at school. If you mention to a schoolteacher that the child's trauma barrier is age three, the teacher will often say, "Oh, you're absolutely right! She acts just like a three-year-old." Let's say this 13-year-old goes to school, gets stressed out, and regresses to the age of 3 emotionally and cognitively. She says, "I can't do my work! I can't do my work!" We might reply, "Well, you did it yesterday! So, I know you can do it today!" When an exchange like this occurs, what does it create for the child? More stress! We need to be present with the child at whatever age the child has reverted to. If a child is acting like a five-year-old, the parent should treat the child like a five-year-old. The parent may say things like "Wow, you're having a hard time" or "Wow, you can't do your work" or "Tell me why you can't do your work." By doing so, an emotional relationship is being established, which is influencing their behavior, and the child will naturally return to the child's developmental age.

THE FOUR LEVELS OF MEMORY

Let's look at the four levels of memory and how each impacts our lives. Take particular note to the State level considered to be the most important because it is believed that trauma impacts the state level of memory. The four levels of memory help parents gain perspective on their child's behaviors.

1. **Cognitive:** Cognitive level of memory involves concepts such as addition, names, phone numbers, addresses, and so on.

2. **Emotional:** Emotional memory involves facial recognition. Emotional memory comes into play when we see someone's face or when we have a feeling or emotion about a person. Don't forget that an emotion and a feeling are different, though. An emotion is what you feel with your body. A feeling, on the other hand, is what you create with your brain through your cognitive process.

3. **Motor:** Motor level of memory is unconscious. This includes activities such as walking, talking, blinking, writing with your ink pen, and scratching your head. Rarely, do we think, "I'm blinking now" because it happens unconsciously. Until we focus our consciousness on the unconscious action, it remains unconscious.

4. **State:** The State level of memory is associated with your brain stem. It develops very early in life. It is believed that the time from conception to the first five years of our lives is the most important for our brain's development and for all of our experiences.

DISSECTING THE STATE LEVEL

Scientists have said that the State Level is the most difficult level of memory to influence and this is true from the traditional perspectives of talk therapy, but when we work from an emotional perspective geared toward the oxytocin response, it isn't true. To influence the state level, we must create learned responses beyond "talking" that will shift us from a cognitive perspective, which is where we parent most often, to an emotional perspective.

STRENGTHENING THE EMOTIONAL PERSPECTIVE: THE MOST INFLUENTIAL PATHWAYS TO A CHILD'S STATE LEVEL OF MEMORY

Facial Expressions: A child seeing a smiling, caring face causes the child to experience a sense and feeling of trust. This sense of trust helps the child to calm a hijacked amygdala, especially when the smiling face has shown themselves to be caring toward the child over time.

Timing: It's best not to address an undesirable behavior at the moment a child is triggered. For example, if a child calls you a name, don't address the name-calling during the child's triggered state. It will only cause more stress for the child. Instead, address the behavior when both the child and parent are calm. This makes timing an important part of addressing a child's state memory.

Intensity: Intensity is important. Sometimes a parent should reflect back to a child with the same intensity of expression or emotion that the child is displaying. For example, if a child is screaming and yelling, the parent can influence the child's state level of memory by reflecting back to the child with the same emotional intensity. Remember that if a parent does this, the parent must use the language of regulation. If the child is yelling things like "I hate you" or "You're a bitch" or "I wish you were dead," the parent should yell back "I love you" or "It makes me sad that someone hurt you so bad that you say those kinds of things. But I'm here to make sure you are safe; I will never leave you."

Tone of voice: Voice tone can help to calm a child's state level of memory depending on the level of the child's triggered state. A calm, soothing voice can help a child feel regulated. In other situations, if the child is so dysregulated that you are not getting their attention, a loud voice using words of regulation (as described above) could be more beneficial in influencing state memory.

Gestures: Gestures are nearly 70% of our communication. Considering this percentage, want to make certain we influence a child using positive open gestures that promote the same response. For example, make a concentrated effort to smile. A smile is welcoming and earns trust. Also, when sitting with the child, maintain open body language. Do not cross your arms or cover your face when speaking.
Crossing your arms demonstrates defensiveness and covering your face indicates that you have something to hide. It could be perceived as lying. In addition, there is eye contact. Eye contact can increase a child's sense of being cared for when the child is developing a trusting relationship with someone.

We have two initial reactions to a frightening event: fight or flight. In the past 30 years, however, scientists have added a third reaction—freeze. Whereas the freeze reaction is new, it's important because it's the first reaction we all have. We freeze before we fight or flee. No one just runs up to somebody and starts fighting. No one automatically runs away. They freeze at first, long enough to perceive the other person as a threat.

So, it's important to understand that when a child perceives a novel event—and any situation for a traumatized child can be a novel event—the freeze reaction is the first response. This might then be followed by fight (anger) or flight (withdrawal), depending on whether the child is hypo-aroused or hyper-aroused. Anger is a survival mechanism because it isn't used to fight and attack, but to push others away.

That's why these children have so much difficulty with transitions from the house to the car, from one classroom to another, or even from the living room to the bathroom. "Everything is a battle," the parent says, and the parent is right.

EXERCISES

On page 33, Bryan refers to a situation where a child is told to get up and walk out the door. Read the story. Then think about a situation where you overreacted. Perhaps you noticed your behavior or perhaps someone else pointed it out to you. Write the story. What do you think might have been the underlying cause of that reaction?

Describe a time that your child overreacted to a simple request. How did you react to the situation? What would you do differently now, understanding the freeze, flight, or fight response?

On page 35, Bryan describes a situation that could have escalated. Please review it. Sam was asked to take out the trash and was given a 5-minute grace period before being asked a second time. Had he not been given this extra time; the situation could have resulted in an escalation. Sam needed time to process—to go from watching television to not watching television. Remember that a child who has experienced trauma can be triggered from a transition.

Chapter 7:

EXPLORING WHAT'S BELOW THE SURFACE

In this section, you will learn:

- Not to ignore below the surface.

"What happens with children is that we label them based on their behaviors as hyperactive, defiant, or aggressive. As soon as we do that, we're guilty of looking only at the tip of the iceberg." Bryan Post.

What we've been talking about since Page 1 is getting below the surface to address the problems. Negative behaviors result from what is going on below the surface.

Review the iceberg story on page 37 of *From Fear to Love*. Bryan compares a child's behavior problems to that of an iceberg. If we were in a boat, we'd see the tip of that iceberg; but we don't see below the surface. And with our adopted child, we fear that the bottom of the iceberg is so big that we will never break through, that we will never reach our adopted child, that the behavior will never improve so we continue to deal with the surface behaviors. This is followed by frustration as things never change. What we must come to accept is complete and utter patience. There is a process—a step by step process that will work. But we must take the steps and follow the process to achieve lasting results.

Describe a situation where you skipped steps. What was the result? Did you have to redo your initial actions? How much did it set you back?

Describe the last time you yelled at your child when they misbehaved. What was the long-term positive behavior change you accomplished?

In life and in business, we want a quick solution. We rush and in doing so, we miss out. With texting, we miss out on communicating with family and friends through phone or in person. We miss out on connecting. We want answers and results immediately. Think about it this way. Long-term training results are accomplished when training is done over time. This means that bits and pieces are discussed, practiced in the classroom, and then taken into the real world to test them. There isn't a quick fix. Long-term change with our adopted child is very similar; we must first find ourselves in a state of regulation so we can get below the surface to bring our child to a state of regulation. When we have accomplished this, both ourselves and our adopted child are in the best position to experience positive change.

There will be ups; there will be downs. There will be successes; there will be failures. But the bottom line is there will be change.

Chapter 8:

The Stress Model

In this section, you will learn:

- The Stress Model and how it will help you as a parent gain a greater understanding of your adopted child.
- The difference between being Reactive Vs. Responsive.

The Stress Model is something we will refer to repeatedly and has been applied to the most severe cases. Its core principle encourages parents to be more Responsive versus Reactive. This is a learned behavior. one that involves continuous learning.

In all its simplicity, the Stress Model™ purports that all behavior arises from a state of stress. Standing between "the behavior" and "the stress" is a primary emotion: love or fear. It is through the expression, the processing, and the understanding
of the fear that we can calm the stress and diminish the behavior. Remember the
11-year-old boy who couldn't stop pooping in his pants? That is a prime example of behavior arising from a state of stress. A parent can make the biggest difference in a child's life when that parent learns how to be responsive rather than reactionary to the child's behavior.

Let's take the example of lying. When a child lies, the parent can respond or react. What is the difference between these two phrases? Had you been the one who lied, how would you have responded to each one?

REACTIVE: "Don't lie to me!"
RESPONSIVE: "Wow, something must be going on with you."

The first response is an example of reactive. It is purely fear-driven. A parent may be fearful because of their own unconscious messages that say my child will not be accepted if they lie, people will think I'm a bad parent, or they cannot succeed in life as an adult if they lie. The second response is an example of responsive, which also involves fear. Responding implies that a parent has calmed their fear to a level they can say things like, "Wow, it seems you are upset about something," instead of reacting, "DON'T LIE TO ME."

Being responsive, however, allows for a cooler head to prevail. To reach the responsive state, the parent might have to talk to himself or herself and say, "I can be calm and respond, and I know that everything is going to be okay." Or "I know my child is in a state. Therefore, I am not going to react in such a way that will cause my child more stress."

A reactive response often occurs because we feel we need to do something immediately. It's a knee-jerk reaction. You take action without completely thinking through the situation. It's totally emotional. Someone might push your buttons and you deliver a quip comment. Someone may not come through for you and you get sarcastic. Have you ever regretted something you said? We all have. The same holds true in business. "Why didn't Susan call the customer. I told her it had to be done first thing in the morning." We're angry. We're disappointed. Then we learn that the customer was out all morning at a doctor's appointment so the call couldn't get made. It's the difference between saying:

REACTIVE: "Susan, if you can't do your job, you're not going to have one!" **RESPONSIVE:** "Susan, were you tied up this morning? I noticed the customer didn't get a call."

We live these reactions every day in one form or another. But with our children, the stakes are higher. We may lash out because we're afraid their behavior might become out of control or perhaps, we're afraid for their future and who they will become or maybe we're even afraid of being labeled a bad parent.

What's the solution? What do we do in these situations?

Here is the 3-Step Formula:

1. Stop. Think to yourself, do you really know "why" your child is behaving the way they are or are you assuming "they're just a bad kid."

2. Take 3 to 10 deep breaths. It sounds so fundamental but allowing oxygen to circulate through our brain and calm us allows for the brain to function most effectively. If you are still angry, put some time and space between you and your child so you can get to a logical place.

3. Respond. This may take the form of a question. "Can I ask you a question?" And when they respond with a "yes," ask, "What happened here?" Or "Are you okay?" You might also comment, "It looks like it's been a tough day for you. What can I do to help?" Any of these responses allows your child to understand that you not only care, but it gives them control of a solution. That's a wonderful thing.

Responding to a child decreases the child's stress state. When parents can consistently respond to a child rather than react to a child, over time, the child learns to feel safe, thus decreasing the impulse to lie. If parents continue to react, then we are causing the child to remain in a fear state, because our reacting is adding to the child's triggered state.

Please reread the story on page 40 of Mahatma Gandhi and his grandson. How would you have reacted if it was your child who lied to you? How did Mahatma Gandhi's response to the situation change your perspective?

What will you do differently moving forward with your adopted child?

Chapter 9:

LYING

In this section, you will learn:

- The Formula to help a child overcome lying.
- Why an adopted child will lie?
- A love-based approach to address lying behavior
- How to bring long-term change.

THE FORMULA

The formula for helping a child overcome lying is to ignore the lie but don't ignore the child. When you ignore the lie, you're ignoring the child's fear and stress state. When a child tells a lie, it comes from a place of sheer terror. They were afraid to tell the truth to you. Every relationship involves at least a second person. You are the second person, and for some reason, your child did not feel comfortable enough to tell you the truth. What was the repercussion of having cookies before dinner?

Why was your child afraid to just say, "Yep, mom, it was me. I took the cookie."

Taking a cookie isn't a big deal. A scolding isn't a big deal. But children with trauma histories lie because for them, it's a life or death situation. These children believe that telling the truth will mean abandonment. So, they have to lie to you, and they cling to the lie out of survival. Their lies are so convincing because their lives depend on those lies. Think of it this way. What happens when you threaten an adopted child's placement because of his/her behavior? "If you don't start acting better, we're going to have to find you another home," or "If this lying doesn't stop, you're out of here"? John Bowlby said, "The threat of loss is equal to loss itself." As soon as you threaten the child, you initiate a grief reaction that elicits fear and stress. You know what comes next—confusion and distortion.

So, when a child tells you she didn't eat the cookie, even though she has crumbs all over her mouth, she's lying to you because she's terrified. Ignoring the lie is difficult for parents because it puts the responsibility back on us as adults.

Because we have our own fear reactions when a child lies, we have to calm ourselves down in this circumstance. Then, we can say something like, "I love you, I care about you, and everything is going to be all right. Do you understand?" You are addressing the child at the heart level. Another comment may be, "Honey, when you lie, it really hurts me, it scares me, and I need you to know that everything is going to be okay." As a parent continues to respond versus react to a child, they will become more and more creative in their feedback to a child.

Always remember the story about Mahatma Gandhi and his grandson. Mahatma felt so bad that his grandson could not tell the truth that he felt he needed to repent. What if, at this moment, we, as parents, took that same responsibility.

What if we asked ourselves, what can I do to strengthen the lines of communication with my adopted child? Or what am I doing that might prevent my adopted child from being truthful? Come from a place of calm, clear thinking, answer these two questions now.

Just as you moved to a place of clarity, we want to enable our child to do the same. When the child moves out of the stress state, her thinking will be clearer, and her short-term memory will become available. That's when he or she will be able to *learn*. REPETITION OF THIS FORMULA IS KEY.

Identify a time you lied. What was the circumstance? Why didn't you tell the truth?

Based on the above comments, had your parent said any of them to you, what would have been your reaction? How would it have opened your mind to truth- based living?

Chapter 10:

STEALING AND SELF-MUTILATION

In this section, you will learn:
- About addictive behaviors like self-mutilation and stealing and how they attempt to soothe an internal state.
- Two quick tips to manage stealing and how to help your child understand the reason he/she steals.
- How to create an environment where the child can express, process, and under- stand the trauma that has caused the stress and leads to the behavior.
- How to use a love-based approach to address the behavior.

Stealing and self-mutilation are addictive behaviors. An addiction is an external attempt to soothe an internal state. When a child steals or cuts himself, it creates a chemical release within the brain and the body, allowing him to feel the relief he needs at the moment. With a traumatized child, concepts of right and wrong, good, and bad, do not register well cognitively because the child is striving to survive emotionally. This survival mechanism is foreign to the child because it is an unconscious process. This is why it is crucial for a child to have parents and caregivers who understand these concepts and ideas for the child, and are willing to do what it takes to help the child process through their emotional challenges, which in time influence the child's behavior, and to some degree their understanding. In this situation, the positive feeling they get from the parent outweighs the trauma feeling. They are now interacting with someone they trust and gravitating toward the positive. This happens unconsciously.

On page 47, Bryan tells the story of a child who enters a Wal-Mart store and steals something. The moment he steals, it feels good to him, and he relaxes. Bryan Post describes the same feeling when he was a child.

What did you learn from those stories?

Did you ever steal? If you did, how did your parents react?

How would you react if your child was to steal?

Knowing what you know about the Old Paradigm, compared to the New Paradigm, how does our reactions to #1 and #2 stunt the growth of our child's behavior?

Let's backtrack a moment. A child that has been in foster care has experienced an extraordinary amount of trauma. Foster Care is not a permanent situation. There may be many moves that prevent the child from healing. Based on the child's past, we really don't know what may spark a reaction and negative behavior from our child. This can create unexpected stress for us, but there can be patterns.

Be observant. When you see a situation where your child is exhibiting negative behavior, note the following.
- What happened prior to the situation?
- What was happening during the situation? Were you out, were there many people around, might it have been an overwhelming situation for your child, what was your child doing? Were they engaged with you prior to the situation or withdrawn?

Everything is important and extremely helpful in anticipating or preventing future situations.

5-Step Process to Stop Your Child from Stealing

1. Recognize your own fears as a parent and self-regulate. Parenting is difficult, especially when we want the best for our child. If we know our child steals, we fear for them, their future, and also our abilities as a parent. As parents, we must realize that we did not cause the stealing. It is not a reflection of us. It is an action, and the more effectively we respond from a neutral regulated place of understanding and love, the faster we will combat the issue.

2. Understand the behavior: The root tip of the behavior is usually a result of the child becoming overwhelmed in a certain environment, for example, a store or public gathering. It causes stress and stealing can calm the stress.

3. Help your child understand why it's happening. Use phrases like: "Honey, you know what? When you go to school, the reason you steal is because you get stressed out and overwhelmed. You feel really scared, don't you? And when you feel really scared, you want to do things that make you feel better. So, you put things in your pockets that don't belong to you. Have you ever thought about that?" Or "Your teacher said you took something that didn't belong to you. You can be hurt by doing that." "Taking from people hurts others. I'm so sorry that I don't make you feel comfortable enough that it causes you to take from others." Creating awareness in a regulated way helps a child better deal with their stress and then opens the door for a child to think about what they're doing when it happens. This is the first step in bringing the change. The child does not know or understand that their behavior results from fear. The parents and/or caregivers must learn and understand the impact trauma has had on the child and become the child's emotional regulator. This is why it is so important for parents and caregivers to have a growing knowledge, understanding, and practice of trauma and self. The better they understand and address their child's emotional state, the more they will enhance the child's abilities to manage their fear state. Children learn to manage their fear state through modeling interaction from regulating parents and caregivers.

4. Create containment in the environment. You might say to your child, "When we go to Wal-Mart, you're going to hold my hand and stay with me. Yes, I know you're 14 years old, but you're going to hold my hand anyway." "Honey, I know when we come to these stores, you get overwhelmed. So, I'm going to have you get in the cart because that way I know that I can keep you safe. We'll both have a very good time here. Okay?" You might have a conversation with your child before going to the store. The conversation should focus on what will take place at the store—whether holding hands, having your child sit in the basket, or having your child walk alongside holding on to the basket. This can be whatever practices you have put in place. When you arrive at the store, ask your child to repeat what will take place.

    If your child becomes dysregulated at the store and cannot follow through, go back to containment, which means leaving the store. Repeating this process will most likely work with repetition.

5. Be on The Lookout. Any severe behavior is usually predictable. If you take the time to watch, you'll usually notice when it happens, what time it happens, how it happens, and what brings it about. You'll see what the child is reacting to, which causes the severe behavior.

SELF-MUTILATION

When we look at self-mutilation, this is also a way to soothe stress. Generally, kids who cut themselves are depressed adolescent girls. When you ask one of these girls why she cuts herself, she's likely to say, "Because it feels good." How can it possibly feel good? But these children feel numb, so when they cut themselves, it feels good for a moment because they feel something. They get a payoff—a release. Angelina Jolie used to cut herself and said in an interview, "I cut myself and just watched the blood run down because it gave me a rush."
So how do we manage the situation.

1. **REGULATE YOURSELF FIRST.** It's not easy for parents to understand why or how a child may do this to themselves, let alone the fact that it feels good. On top of this and most challenging is that no parent can handle any physical trauma their child may experience. And now they are watching their child do this to themselves.

2. **TELL YOUR CHILD "THE WHY"**: Just as with stealing, bring the reasons for the cutting into the child's consciousness. You can say, "You cut yourself when you feel really stressed out and scared." "Wow, what's going on? What happened?" What you're doing here is helping her to make an emotional connection and creating an environment for the child to express, process, and understand the trauma that caused this behavior. That will begin to help her stop the cutting behavior.

3. **TELL YOUR CHILD'S STORY.** If you know the details of the trauma, you can create the narrative for the child. Hold her in your arms, and tell her, "When you were a little girl, this happened, and it was really scary for you. And that's why you cut yourself." Once again, creating that emotional connection helps the child to process and understand. That will begin the process for her to stop cutting.

4. **REINFORCE YOUR SUPPORT.** As difficult as it may be to do, tell your child, "Cut yourself if you need to, but I would really like for you to come and tell me when you feel like you need to cut yourself. Come to me before you do it." Your goal is to be present when it happens so you can reduce your child's stress by responding rather than reacting, by approaching the situation from a regulated space. If your child spends time with you, and you offer her comfort and support, she will calm down. Eventually, she might not feel the need to cut herself. Can you imagine that? It's the power of taking that unconscious experience and making it conscious. As soon as you do that, the pain from the cutting intensifies, and it stops feeling so good. She will cut herself and will be more aware of what's happening. Suddenly, she'll think, "I'm cutting myself. Ouch!" She's no longer so numb.

PHRASES TO AVOID

"Don't cut yourself. It isn't right!" "How could you do that?" "What's the matter with you?"

Remember, if you cannot regulate yourself, you will not be in the best position to help your child. Self-mutilation is scary, but to your child, this is the only way she knows how to deal with the stress and the fear.

Other than your child, do you know someone who was a "cutter?" How did you respond to the situation?

Should you come across someone who "cuts", knowing what you know now, what steps would you take to help them?

What are some things you would do if your child was a "cutter?"

What does this experience teach you about trauma and children, in general?

Chapter 11:
AGGRESSIVE BEHAVIOR

In this section, you will learn:

That aggressive behaviors result from a child perceiving an event as a threat

Aggressive behaviors include but are not limited to yelling and screaming, cursing, throwing things, breaking things, punching, and kicking walls, and attacking a person or animal.

If you walk past me, and I can't perceive in the moment that you're safe, I will immediately perceive you as a threat. If I'm an adopted child without the ability to determine that I'm not threatened in what others would consider a safe situation, I might hit you as you walk past me. It's an impulsive act. If your child is on the playground at school. Another kid is running past him and not even playing with him, and your child trips or bites this kid. Your child could not perceive this other kid wasn't a threat.

Children who do cruel things are reenacting an early trauma; this may include children who harm animals. I have worked with children who have starved an animal because they were chronically neglected and not given enough food in the past. These children are trying to work through the trauma and are not aware of what they're doing. Let me explain. A child traumatized is a child in survival mode constantly. Trauma causes confused, distorted, and irrational thinking. The emotional pain that a traumatized child is experiencing could cause them to create irrational ways of dealing with their emotional pain. The child, in some misunderstood way of reasoning, could think that by starving the animal, it could, in some way, help them through their trauma experience. The brain and soul of a chronically traumatized child and adults can cause bizarre ways of thinking to find some relief from their trauma state.

A child who has difficulties with others, especially peers, is a child who has regressed to a younger emotional age. The child's social skills suffer. Stress research indicates that when we encounter high levels of stress, our body cells constrict into survival. In that situation, we cannot have a conscience because in high stress levels, the only thing we can focus on is our own survival.

A child is about to get sent home from school due to excessive talking in class. The teacher doesn't realize that the child is answering a student's question. The teacher asks the child if the child was talking. Just then, fear is triggered with the child— fear of punishment, detention, and whatever other trauma has been triggered. The child immediately says, "No." At that moment, due to fear, the child could not explain the situation to the teacher, so the child lied. The child could not act with a conscience. That's why these children seem to have no conscience, but this is a huge misconception. When they become regulated and are no longer in survival mode, they do indeed have a conscience. In the example above, the child knows the teacher saw her talking, but the child lies. To the teacher, the child is being defiant, lacking respect and/or lacks consciousness of right or wrong, good, and bad.

Now, once the situation became regulated, the teacher went to the student and asked if the student was okay and if there was anything she would like to talk about. Since the child is not regulated, the child felt comfortable enough to explain to the teacher what had taken place.

If a child experienced abuse, the behavior might be a distorted way of trying to heal their trauma.

What is an aggressive behavior that your child is exhibiting?

What trauma has your child experienced in the past?

Is your child aware of what has happened to them? What can you do to provide an environment where they can process the events?

What are some things you can do to see your child's behavior from a different perspective?

Chapter 12:

WHAT DO CHRONIC LYING, STEALING, FIRE-SETTING, KILLING ANIMALS, AND HOARDING FOOD HAVE IN COMMON?

In this section, you will learn:

- The main premise of Reactive Attachment Disorder (RAD) and that the child cannot form positive, lasting relationships.
- When RAD will have the greatest impact on a child.
- The results of RAD and trust issues.
- The potential for healing and RAD.

BONDING DISORDER

Reactive Attachment Disorder is a myth. As long as a child is in a state of stress and fear, he cannot develop secure attachment. As long as the parents are in states of fear and stress, they can't bond with the child, either. Kennel and Klaus, the pioneering attachment pediatricians, say, "Attachment is the behavior from the child to the parent, and bonding is the behavior from the parent to the child." Attachment and bonding is a two-way street. We can't focus on a child's ability to attach without focusing on the parents' ability to bond, because if the parent also has a trauma history, he/she will have an impaired ability to bond as well. Many parents grew up with parents who had impaired attachment abilities, so their own parents were both prone to dysregulation, making it difficult to engage their child's oxytocin response. Here are a few steps parents can take to help a child who struggles with emotional attachment: become trauma-informed, attend a trauma-informed conference and/or see a therapist, and above all, do the personal work so that as a parent you can better understand what your child is going through emotionally and how their behaviors are affected by the disorder. Also, please remember that there are things you can do to support your child's growth process—maintain a structured environment, set limits, be consistent in your words and actions, establish predictability, and demonstrate affection often.

Describe the environment in which you grew up? Were your parents emotional present for you? Were your parents in a state of regulation or dysregulation?

How has that environment affected you as a parent? Have you adopted some of the same methodologies as your parents?

Does your child exhibit extreme behaviors?

What steps will you take daily to help your child regulate?

Chapter 13:
FEEDBACK LOOPS

In this section, you will learn:

- How to recognize feedback loops and impact your child's behavior.
- That every family has a rhythmic relationship with one another, and if one family member is dysregulated, every family member is dysregulated.
- The importance of never using fear, threats, or isolation when addressing challenging behaviors, or you risk creating a negative feedback loop resulting in the family's dysregulation
- The power of one well-regulated person to contain a negative feedback loop.

According to the Stress Model™, Parental regulation is ultimately the single most important factor in the development of successful independent regulatory functioning in children." Nothing makes as big a difference as a regulated parent does. The parent's own state of regulation will help to bring the child from dysregulation to regulation.

When we communicate with one another, we create a feedback loop. If we use fear, threats, or isolation with our child, we will create a negative physiologic feedback loop.
The below Negative Feedback Loop appears in the From Fear to Love book on the bottom of Page 64. It is a classic negative neurophysiologic feedback loop and an example of pure fear. Notice the title at the beginning of each line.

ORDER: Parent: "Take out the trash."
          Child: "No, I'm not going to."
          A feedback loop has just begun.

ORDER: Parent: "I said to take out the trash!" (The loop gets bigger)
          Child: "No, I'm not going to!"

THREAT: Parent: "You're going to do it because I said so!"
          Child: "I don't care what you say!"

THREAT: Parent: "Don't talk to me like that!"
          Child: "I'll talk to you any way I want!"

THREAT: Parent: "You just wait until your dad gets home, and we'll see what happens!"

COGNITIVE BEHAVIOR PARENTING TOOLS:

Below, please find 95% of the tactics we use with children, but they only address the behavior and what's on the surface. They don't address the state level, and they're all fear based.

- Boot-camp tactics
- Jumping jacks
- Excessive chores
- Isolation
- Behavior modification
- Money and bribery
- Point charts
- Toys and trips
- Logic and reasoning consequences
- Spanking
- Yelling
- Choices

POSITIVE FEEDBACK LOOPS.

Below please find an example of creating a *positive* feedback loop.

REQUEST Parent: "Honey, I need you to take out the trash."
Child: "No, I'm not going to!"

QUESTION Parent: "Wow, what's going on?"
(The parent is responding rather than reacting.)
Child: "I don't care what you tell me."

REAFFIRM Parent: "Something must really be bothering you."
Child: "Nothing's bothering me."

REAFFIRM Parent: "Well, I know if something weren't bothering you, you wouldn't be talking to me that way. You'd be calmer, and you'd take out the trash."

TAKE A BREAK IF NECESSARY

FOLLOW UP Parent: "Can we talk about what just happened?"

Have you ever had an experience with someone who was angry, but you calmed the person down because you were in a good mood? We all have at one point or an- other. Let's take this same approach with our children. If the parent has remained regulated, they have contained the child's negative feedback loop. A parent in a regulated state will be more responsive and able to acknowledge that their child is in a triggered state. The parent is then in a space to use the words necessary to meet the child where they are emotionally.

How would you describe your interaction with your parents? Was it more like the first conversation or the second conversation?

Based on the second conversation, what will you say differently to your child?

Chapter 14:

THE 3-PHASE INTERVENTION

In this section, you will learn:

- The Three-Phase Intervention: Reflect, Relate, Regulate.
- How to incorporate the Three-Phase Intervention into your life.
- How Reflect, Relate, Regulate creates a positive feedback loop in the middle of chaos.

Creating a positive feedback loop can be as simple as using the Three-Phase Intervention. It consists of Reflect-Relate-Regulate. Take a few minutes and read the two stories beginning at the bottom of Page 69—one involves a child who acted out when they were to take a bath and the other involved a child who acted out prior to a shower. In both these instances, they were instructed to Reflect. Relate. Regulate.

Let's look at each step:
1. Reflect: Take 3-10 deep breaths. Inhale through your nose and exhale through your mouth. Get in touch with your own fear.

2. Relate to your child. You can even say to the child, "I feel really scared right now. Tell me how you're feeling." Tell the child how you're feeling before asking him how he's feeling. Otherwise, he might perceive a threat from you.

3. Regulate: In taking these steps, you begin to *regulate yourself*, your child, and the environment.

It is very important that during this process, you allow your child to feel whatever they are feeling—anger, fear, sadness. These are their feelings, allow them.

Let's say, for example, that you say to your child, "I feel scared. How do you feel?" Your child says, "I'm mad!" You might then say, "If you're mad, tell me about it. Yell it out! Let me have it!" You know how scary yelling is in our society. Any expression of emotion frightens us. We say, "Don't! Shhhh!" Our impulse is to immediately push it down. As soon as you give the child permission to let you know exactly how he feels, he will regulate.

These steps are the same, whether it's the father or the mother involved. Reflect-Relate-Regulate!

Describe a situation where you could have implemented Reflect, Relate, Regulate. Looking back, how would you have handled the process today?

Situation:

Reflect:

Relate:

R
Regulate:

Chapter 15:

HEALING HAPPENS AT HOME

In this section, you will learn:

- Powerful prescriptions for dealing with your child's behaviors.
- You are in control of the healing process, not another person, therapist, book, or article.
- What is mindfulness and how can we make mindfulness the essence of our life.
- What is Reflect, Relate, Regulate?
- Three examples of in-home healing that demonstrate the New Parenting Paradigm.

As progressive parents, we invest in books, classes, any form of education that will help us be better in life, in business and in the home. From Fear to Love supports these efforts, just as any therapist would guide you through a process to create peace in your life. Ultimately, we want you to have the tools you need to bring a healing environment to your ho1me. Bryan Post's goal is to educate parents, help them understand, bring awareness, give them insight, and help them to create an environment for their children to understand, gain awareness, and be given insight. There is no perfect plan; we can only do the very best we can.

Mindfulness
A strong supporting character in From Fear to Love is "mindfulness." Mindfulness is the ability to slow down enough to watch your own thoughts, sensations, perceptions, and behaviors. It's almost like stepping outside of yourself and observing yourself. Through mindfulness, you make the unconscious conscious.

It is one of the most important tools a parent can use to maintain their own state of calm and regulation, and thereby better influence and parent their children.

EXERCISE

Dr. Jon Kabat-Zinn, one of the leading mindfulness researchers, says that "mindfulness means **paying attention** in a particular way; **on purpose**, in the **present moment,** and **non-judgmentally.**" Describe the last time in your life you acted in accordance with Dr. Jon Kabat-Zinn's definition of mindfulness?

What was the situation?

How did you pay attention on purpose?

How did you pay attention in the present moment?

How did you pay attention non-judgmentally?

REFLECT, RELATE REGULATE

Bryan Post's mindfulness prescription helps you move into the present – which is the best place to parent from – with my *3 Steps to Peace: Fostering Love in the Midst of Fear*. Next time you are feeling dysregulated with your child's behavior, try the 3R's - 3 Steps to Peace:

1) **REFLECT:** Stop and take 3-5 deep breaths and ask yourself how you are feeling.

2) **RELATE:** Accept your feelings as OK (whatever they are—non-judgmentally). Tell your child, "I am feeling____. What are you feeling?

3) **REGULATE:** Seek to understand. Not only hear, but listen to what is being said and what is *not* being said. Continue to breathe and relate. Regulation, like love will happen naturally. Scott Rogers states in his book *Mindful Parenting*, it's not about raising your child, it's about you and me: "When we are mindful, we see what is before us; when we are not, we see what is in our mind."

EXERCISE:

Describe the last time you incorporated Bryan Post's mindfulness prescription into your life with your adopted child.
What was the situation and how did you do the following?

Reflect:

Relate:

Regulate:

IN-HOME HEALING OPPORTUNITIES

Below are practices you can incorporate into your everyday life that will help you live from a place of regulation.

TIME-IN VERSUS TIME-OUT

Time-out does not recognize the developmental and regulatory struggles children demonstrate during their acting out behavior. Consider for a moment that rather than a child acting out "for" attention, *she is acting out because she "needs" attention.*

Instead of sending the child off to sit in a chair or be isolated, bring the child close to you for a period. Have her sit next to you, hold your hand, or stand beside you. Say to the child, "When you're feeling better, you can go back and play." Allow the child to determine how much time-in she needs. This process has been determined to be 95% effective where children will stay in time-in longer than they will stay in time-out.

When was the last time you put time-in to use? What happened? What was the result?

What is your plan for continuing the time-in process? Include where you may be likely to incorporate time-in. At home? When you are out? How will you incorporate it into your everyday life?

What were your child's thoughts of time-in? Ask them.

Containment

Containment is an expanded form of time-in. It involves decreasing the space in which the child feels threatened. You can do this by not allowing the children to go upstairs during the day. Close doors and create a space in the living room or some other room, allowing for more regulation for the children. As long as they're close to you and can see you, they will feel more regulated. If they feel more regulated, they won't be as likely to get into trouble.

When was the last time you practiced containment with your adopted child? What did you notice about their behavior—positive or negative—as a result?

What will you do to continue this process in your everyday life?

Affection Prescription

The affection prescription consists of the concept of Ten-Twenty-Ten. Give your child 10 minutes of quality time and interaction first thing in the morning. Just spend time with the child, put your arm around her, talk to her softly (I prefer that you not even talk), sit with the child in your lap and rock her or hum to her. Then, immediately after school or when you get home from work, sit down with her on the couch for 20 minutes. Ask her about her day. Spend 20 minutes of uninterrupted, undivided attention. Then, spend another 10 minutes with her in the evening.

When was the last time you used the Affection Prescription? What was the situation?

What adjustments did you make, or will you make regarding time so you can make this part of your daily routine?

What benefits did you notice with your child after the Affection Prescription practice was used?

FROM FEAR TO LOVE - Conclusion

Based on the book *From Fear To Love*, what four things will you incorporate into your day-to-day life with your child?

1.

2.

3.

4.

Post Test

1. The difference between the Old Paradigm and the New Paradigm is:
a. There is no Old or New Paradigm, there is just parenting, and we all operate differently doing whatever we think is best.
b. The Old Paradigm states that you learned how to parent from your parents and grandparents and the New Paradigm means that you are creating your own new formula for parenting.
c. The Old Paradigm states that you as a parent were in charge and the New Paradigm means that your child is now in charge.
d. The Old Paradigm states that the child is angry and controlling and that as a parent, you are operating from a place of punishment and control; and the New Paradigm means that you, as a parent, are operating from a place of understanding, flexibility, and acceptance.

2. The two primary emotions we feel as human beings are:
a. Love and Anger
b. Love and Hate
c. Love and Fear
d. Love and Jealousy

3. When an adopted child gets stressed:
a. The stress exhausts the child and causes the child to become tired and sleepy.
b. The stress causes confused and distorted thinking and suppresses short-term memory, which then drives negative behavior.
c. The stress causes the child to become clingy.
d. The stress causes the child and parent to immediately come to an understanding, leading to improved behavior.

4. According to the National Institute of Mental Health, stress is:
a. Important to maintain a balanced lifestyle.
b. How the brain and body respond to any demand.
c. A result of our eating habits.
d. Necessary to better manage the behaviors of our children.

5. Stress is ____ and ____ in life.
a. Avoidable and unnecessary
b. Scary and unnecessary
c. A challenge and important
d. Unavoidable and necessary

6. Trauma may occur as early as _____.
a. When a child learns their first words.
b. When a child is first reprimanded.
c. When a child is born.
d. When a child begins to socialize at school.

7. True or False: Trauma is any stressful event that is prolonged, overwhelming, or unpredictable, and when that event continues unexpressed, unprocessed, and misunderstood, it becomes long-term trauma.

8. One step of the healing process is to encourage a conversation with your child. The other two steps are:
a. Listening to your child and then holding them.
b. Explaining to your child the way they should respond and gaining agreement.
c. Explaining to your child why they are reacting badly and brainstorming ideas to improve.
d. Listening to their thoughts and then disciplining through chores.

9. This part of the brain contributes to calming stress and helping a child think more clearly and feel less overwhelmed.
a. Amygdala
b. Hippocampus
c. Orbitofrontal Cortex
d. Sensory Pathway

10. This part of the brain is fully developed at by the time an infant reaches 18 months of age. Therefore, the infant's ability to sense threats, fear, and stress is functioning
a. Amygdala
b. Hippocampus
c. Oxytocin
d. Orbitofrontal Cortex

11. True or False. Oxytocin is called the anti-stress hormone and, sometimes, the bonding hormone because of its power to soothe.

12. Examples of Attuned and Attentive Caregiving, required to initiate the oxytocin response, include all of the following except:
a. Listening
b. Hugging
c. Playing
d. Ignoring

13. True or False: The oxytocin response is a learned response.

14. True or False: During a time of stress, a child will emotionally revert to an early experience of trauma or the "trauma core."

15. True or False: The State Level is the most difficult level of memory to influence according to traditional perspectives of talk therapy, but when we work from an emotional perspective geared toward the oxytocin response; it isn't true. To influence the State Level, we must create learned responses beyond "talking" that will shift us from a cognitive perspective, to an emotional perspective.

16. The most influential pathways to a child's State Level include all of the following except:
a. Smiling, seeing a caring face causes the child to experience a sense and feeling of trust.
b. Addressing an undesirable behavior at the moment a child is triggered
c. Reflecting back to a child with the same voice and tone intensity of expression or emotion that the child is displaying.
d. Voice tone, which can help to calm a child's state level of memory depending on the level of the child's triggered state.

17. True or False. Regulation helps you to stay calm and focused. It enables you to manage your emotions, minimizing your fears and creating understanding with your child.

18. True or False. Dysregulation is the body's state of stress outside the window of tolerance. Dysregulation is a place where you see things clearly and translate thoughts in a lucid, practical manner.

19. True or False. The Stress Model™ purports that all behavior arises from a state of stress. It is through the expression, the processing, and the understanding of the fear that we can calm the stress and diminish the behavior.

20. The 3-Step Formula to Respond Vs React includes all of the following except:
a. Stop and think. Do you know why your child is behaving the way they are?
b. Assume the reason for the negative behavior based on previous experience.
c. Take 3 to 10 deep breaths.
d. Respond either with a question or statement

21. True or False. The formula for helping a child overcome lying is to ignore the lie but don't ignore the child because when you ignore the lie, you're ignoring the child's fear and stress state.

22. True or False. Learning occurs when the child moves out of the stress state, their thinking is clearer, and their short-term memory becomes available.

23. True or False. Stealing and self-mutilation are not addictive behaviors

24. A primary step in managing self-mutilation behavior is to reinforce your support by doing all of the following except:
a. Saying, "Cut yourself if you need to, but I would really like for you to come and tell me when you feel like you need to cut yourself so I can be there for you."
b. Being physically and mentally present when it happens to reduce the child's stress.
c. Coming from a place of understanding and listening.
d. Asking the child, "What's the matter with you?" This will force the child to stop.

25. Aggressive behaviors include all of the following except:
a. Sharing your feelings.
b. Cursing.
c. Punching and kicking walls.
d. Attacking a person or animal.

26. True or False. As long as a child is in a state of stress and fear, he cannot develop secure attachment. As long as the parents are in states of fear and stress, they can't bond with the child. Attachment and bonding are a two-way street.

27. True or False. According to the Stress Model™, parental regulation is ultimately the single most important factor in the development of successful independent regulatory functioning in children to bring the child from dysregulation to regulation.

28. All of the following are examples of Cognitive Behavior Parenting Tools, except:
a. Excessive
b. Chores
c. Isolation
d. Listening

29. Which of the following is NOT an example of a Negative Feedback Loop?
a. "You're going to do it because I said so!"
b. "Don't you talk to me like that!"
c. "Wow, what's going on here?"
d. "You just wait until your dad gets home, and we'll see what happens!"

30. Which is not an example of a parenting response from a Positive Feedback Loop:
a. "Wow, what's going on?"
b. "Misbehaving isn't going to solve this."
c. "Something must really be bothering you."
d. "Can we talk about what just happened here

31. One way to create a Positive Feedback Loop is:
a. Reflect, Relate Regulate
b. Reflect, Remember, Relate
c. Peace, Love, and Harmony
d. Research, Remember, Recover

32. The steps of the Positive Feedback Loop include all of the following except:
a. Reflect: Take 3-10 deep breaths
b. Remember your objective.
c. Relate to your child.
d. Regulate yourself, your child, and the environment.

33. True or False. Mindfulness is one of the most important tools a parent can use to maintain their own state of calm and regulation to better influence and parent a child. It is the ability to slow down enough to watch your own thoughts, sensations, perceptions, and behaviors.

34. In-home healing opportunities include all of the following except:
a. Time In Versus Time Out
b. Containment
c. Affection Prescription
d. Regulate

www.ingramcontent.com/pod-product-compliance
Lightning Source LLC
Chambersburg PA
CBHW042007150426
43195CB00002B/49